learning. exploring. discovering. learning.

USA

Children's travel activity and keepsake book

learning. exploring. discovering. learning. exploring. discovering. learning. exploring. discovering.

tinytourists

explore. discover. learn.

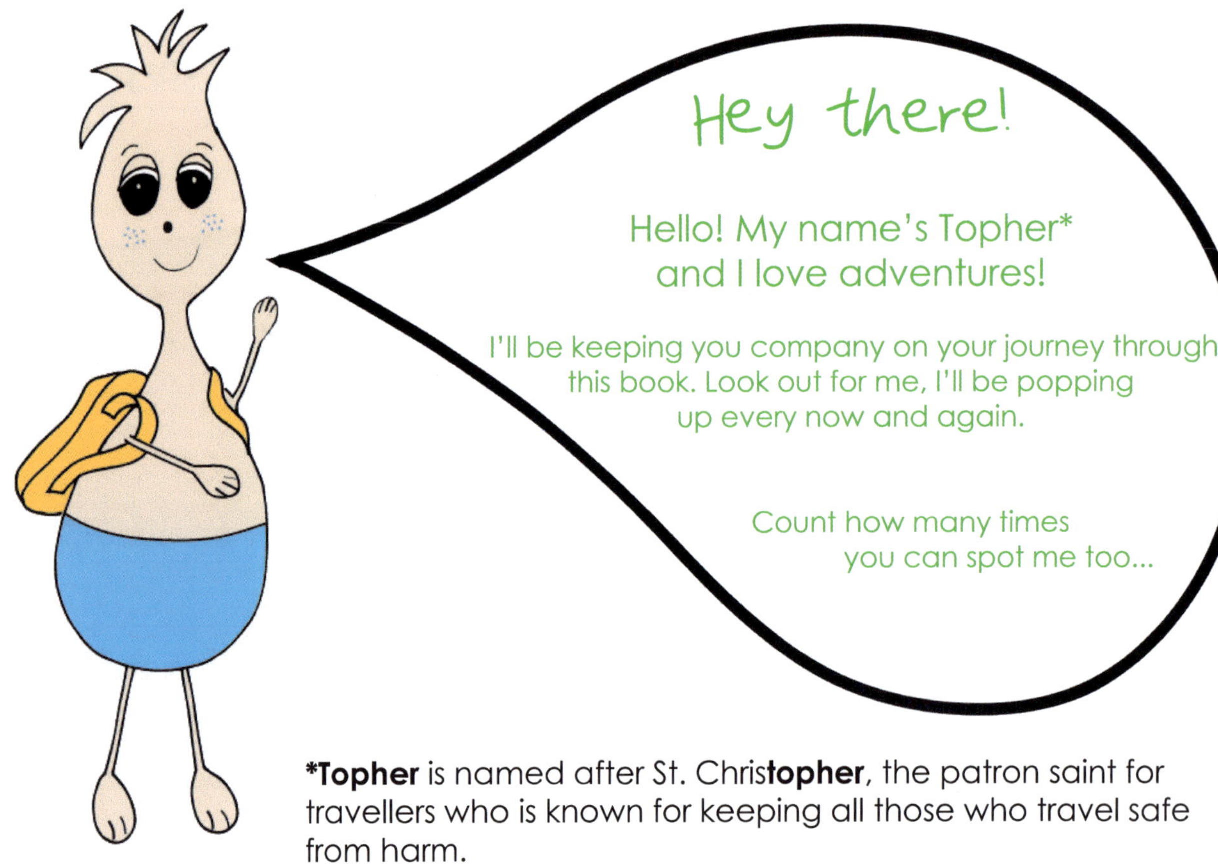

***Topher** is named after St. Chris**topher**, the patron saint for travellers who is known for keeping all those who travel safe from harm.

Visit us at www.tinytourists.co.uk to receive our FREE monthly newsletter full of tips, travel advice and inspiration for more family adventures!

tinytourists is all about inspiring family travel and making the most of adventures; keeping travel meaningful and memorable, educational and fun. Visit our website, and find us on Facebook to join our community of travel-parents.

Written and Designed by Louise Amodio
Illustrated by Louise Amodio and Catherine Mantle
Cover Illustrations by Giacomo (age 8), Emma (5), and Francesca (8) and Greta (7).

Published by Beans and Joy Publishing Ltd as a product from Tiny Tourists Ltd, Great Britain.
www.tinytourists.co.uk

ISBN: 978-0-9954949-3-0

This belongs to:

Your adventure starts here

How to use this book

Welcome to your fun-packed travel activity book!

Look out for these symbols to tell you what type of activity you'll be doing so you can start to work independently:

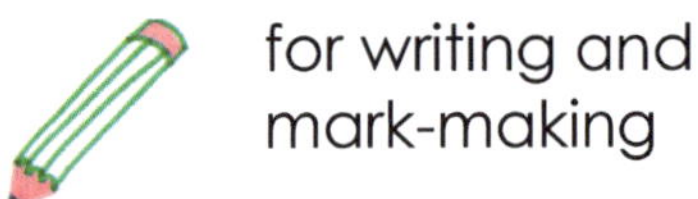

for writing and mark-making

for drawing and colouring and being creative

Section 1: My Travel Log

Use this section to start thinking about your trip to the USA; when you're going, where you're going, who you're going with, what the weather be like, and what you'll pack in your suitcase. This will help form part of a lovely keepsake as well as practice your planning and organisational skills!

Section 2: Explorer Skills

This section is full of games and activities for a bit of USA-themed fun. All are designed to support the National Curriculum and are grouped into **Maths (p12-25)**, **Literacy (p26-36), and The World Around Us (p37-42)**. See the index for details.

Section 3: Memory Bank

This is where you can record all the memories from your trip. The perfect finishing touch to a lovely book of holiday memories; what you did, what you ate, what you saw, what you collected, and fun lists for recording the best bits and the worst bits.

Happy Travels!

My Travel Log

Stick or draw your picture here

Me:

My Destination:

Arrival:

Date: ____________

Passport Stamp:

Departure:

Date: ____________

Where am I going?

This is a map of the United States of America (USA).

Find out where you are going on holiday, any journeys you may be taking, and add them to the map:

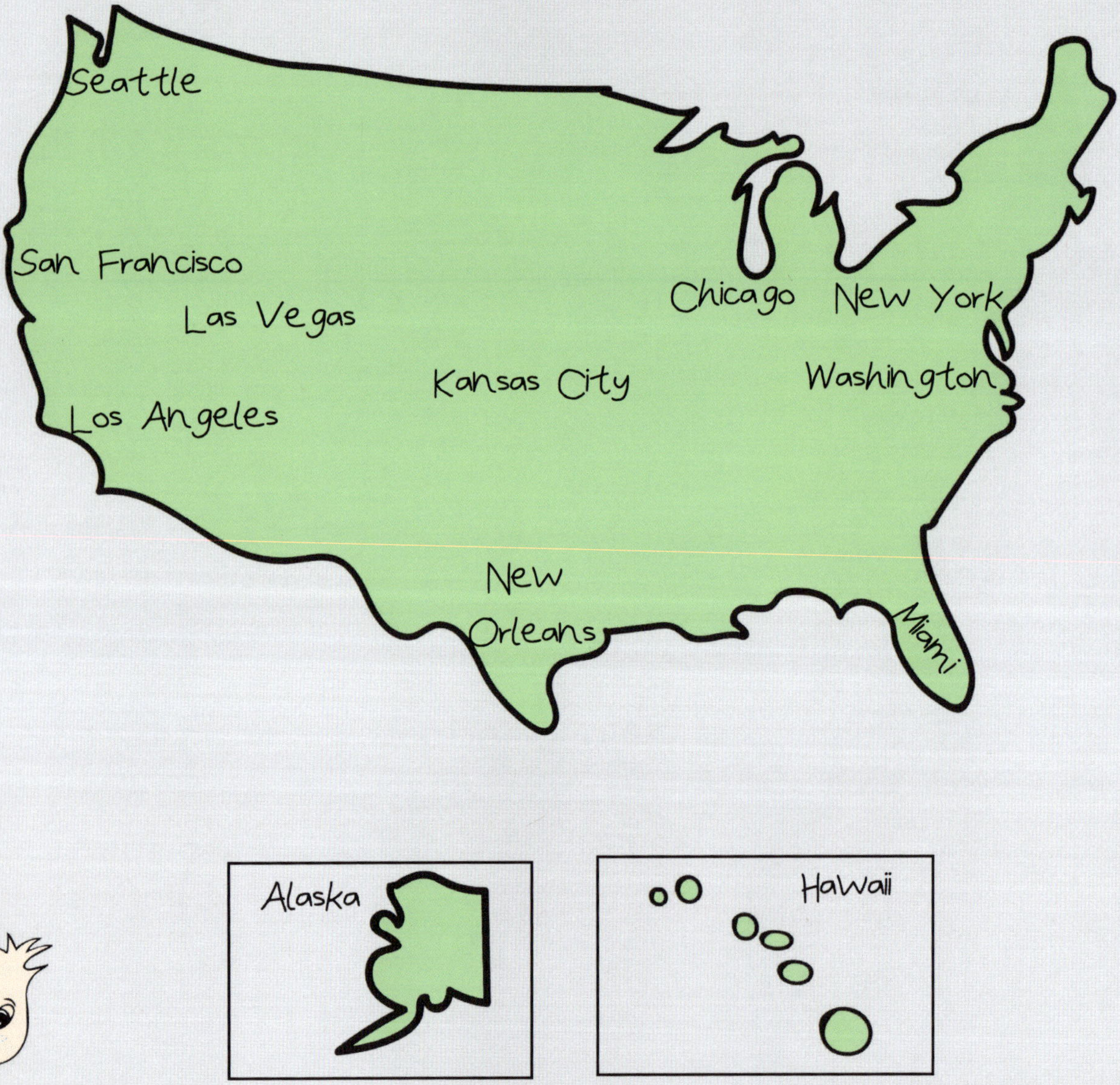

Seattle

San Francisco

Las Vegas

Los Angeles

Kansas City

Chicago

New York

Washington

New Orleans

Miami

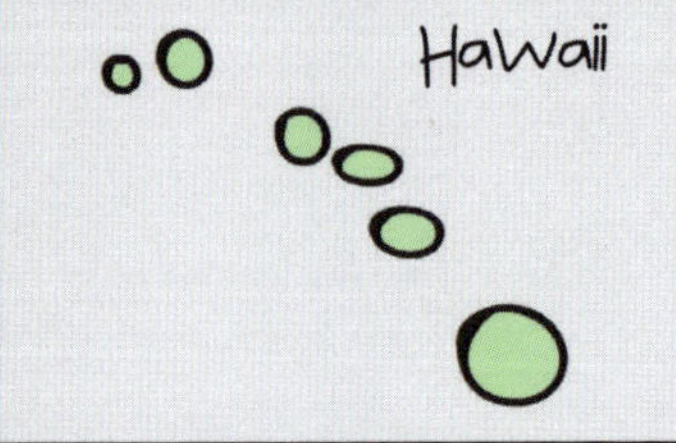

Not to scale

How will I get there?

Find the transport you're using to get to the USA and colour it in:

What am I taking with me?

Draw the important things you've got packed in your suitcase:

Who am I going with?

Draw a picture of who you're going on holiday with in the frame below:

Holiday Portrait

What will the weather be like?

Draw a circle around the weather you think you'll have:

Explorer Skills

Problem-solving
(Maths)

Code-breaking
(Literacy)

Spy Skills
(The World
Around Us)

The Stars and Stripes

This is the American flag, with 13 stripes and 50 stars.

Complete the flag below by colouring in the red stripes:

Red Corvettes

Circle all the **red** Corvette cars.

How many are there?

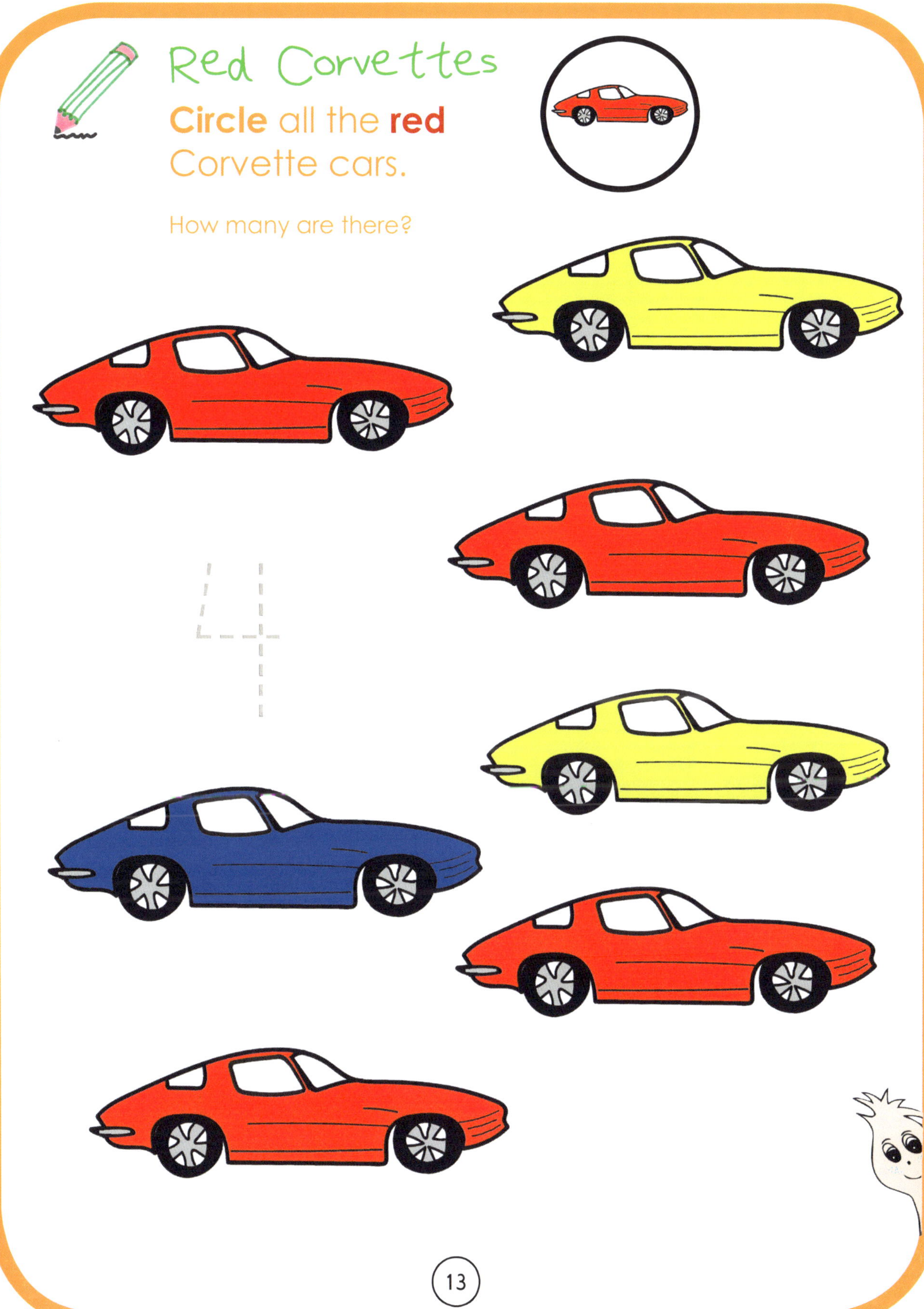

Blue Cadillacs

Circle all the **blue** Cadillac Cars

How many are there?

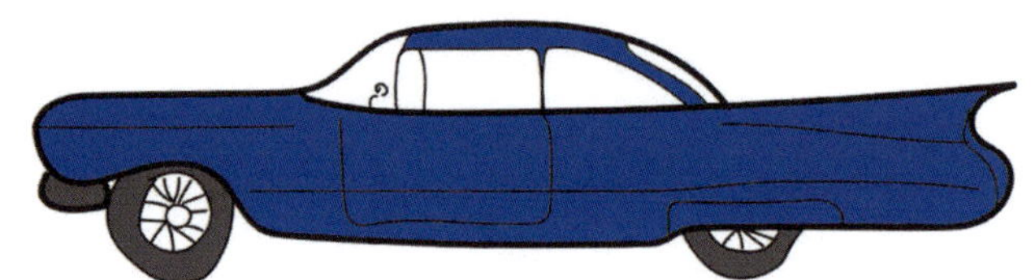

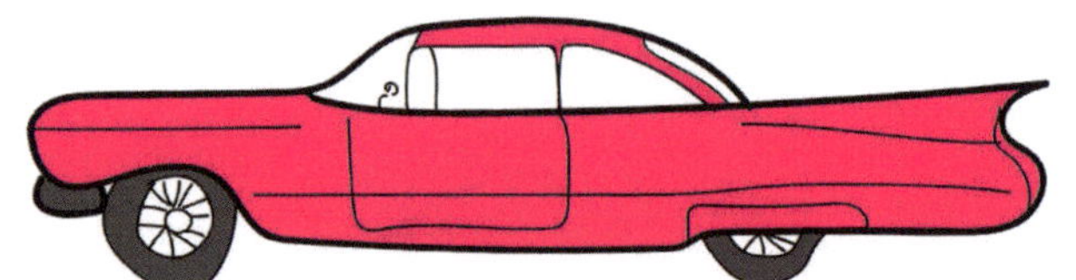

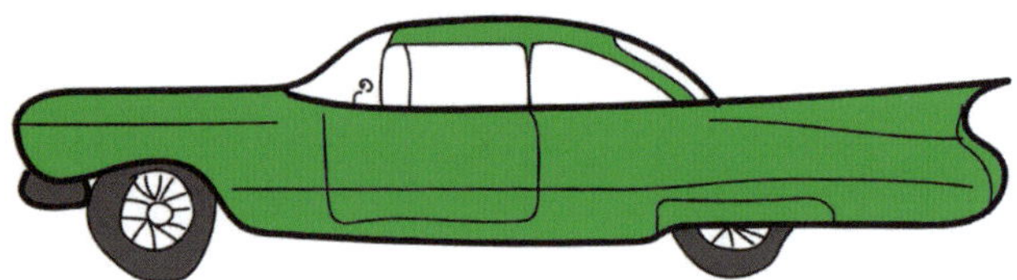

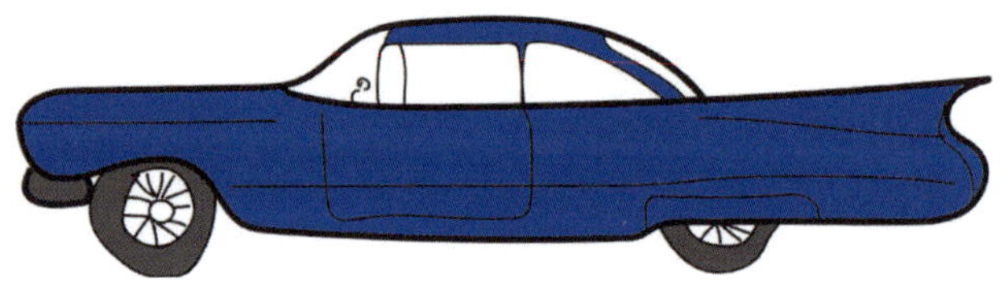

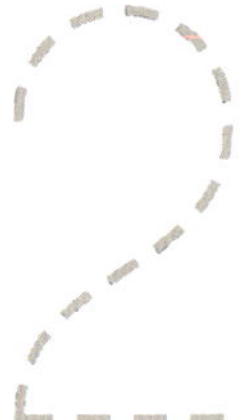

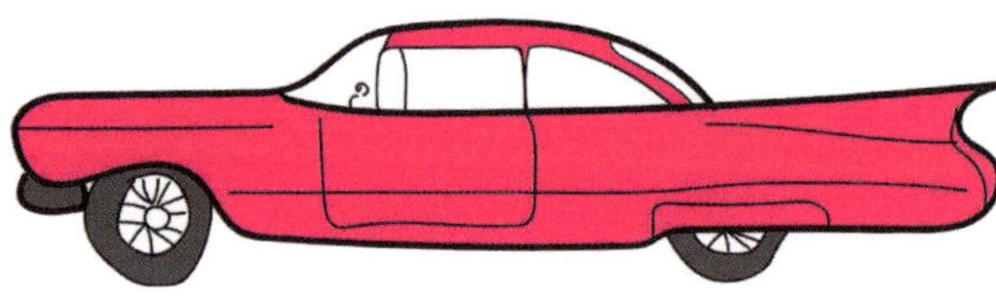

Monster Truck

You may spot a monster truck on your travels. See if you can **copy the colours** and add some colour to the big monster truck below:

Fast Food 1-5

Burgers, Fries, Hot Dogs and Pizza are very popular in America and you will probably see lots of different fast food restaurants on your travels.

Count the fast food items below and circle the right number on the number line:

1 2 3 4 5

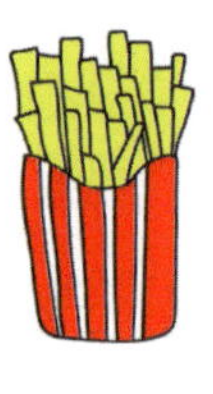

1 2 3 4 5

1 2 3 4 5

1 2 3 4 5

Fast Food 1-10

Count the food and **circle the right number** below.
Which one do you think is your favourite?
Do you think this food is healthy or not healthy?

1 2 3 4 5 6 7 8 9 10

1 2 3 4 5 6 7 8 9 10

1 2 3 4 5 6 7 8 9 10

1 2 3 4 5 6 7 8 9 10

Desserts 1-5

You will probably get to try many delicious America desserts on your travels.

Count the Cheesecakes, Choc Chip Cookies, Apple Pies and Ice-Cream Sundaes below and **circle the right number** on the number line:

1 2 3 4 5

1 2 3 4 5

1 2 3 4 5

1 2 3 4 5

Desserts 1-10

Count these desserts and **circle the right number** below. Which one do you think is your favourite? Do you think this food is healthy or not healthy?

1 2 3 4 5 6 7 8 9 10

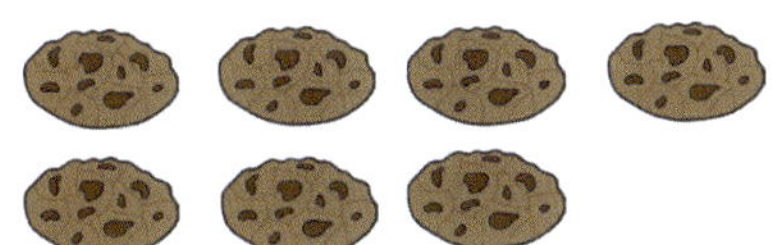

1 2 3 4 5 6 7 8 9 10

1 2 3 4 5 6 7 8 9 10

1 2 3 4 5 6 7 8 9 10

Sundae Fun

What is your favourite flavour of ice-cream?

Colour in the Sundae using your favourite colours:

Diner Matching Pairs

A visitor to an American Diner orders two of everything on the menu. **Draw a line between each matching pair** below to help the chef make sure enough food has been prepared:

American Black Bears

Black Bears are the most common type of bear that live in America. They often live in mountains and forests. They love to eat nuts, berries, fish and small mammals.

See if you can **find the smallest bear** on this mountain:

FACT!
"Black Bears" can actually have brown, white, cinnamon or cream fur coats.

Smallest Bear

Circle the smallest bear in each row:

America's National Bird

America's national bird and national animal is the Bald Eagle. You might spot them in the mountains and by the sea where they try to catch fish.

Can you **find the biggest eagle** in these moutains and draw a circle around it?

FACT! Bald Eagles are not actually bald. They have white feathers on their heads.

Biggest Eagle

Can you **circle the biggest eagle** on each row:

The White House

The President of the United States of America lives in The White House in Washington.

Use your colouring pencils to **add some colour** to this picture, and maybe add some sky, a garden, flowers and fountains:

The Statue of Liberty

The Statue of Liberty is one of America's most famous monuments, It was a gift from France to celebrate the 100th year of American Independence. It stands on Liberty Island, in New York.

Use your colouring pencils to **add some colour to this picture.**
Lady Liberty's torch is coated in gold, and her dress is green.

FACT!
Visitors can climb up inside the Statue. There are 354 steps that take you up to the crown.

American Football

Three of the most popular sports in America are baseball, basketball and American football.

In the maze below, **draw a line** from the football all the way to the goal area to get a touchdown:

END ZONE

Baseball

Can you **draw round the dotted line** to score a Home Run on this baseball pitch?

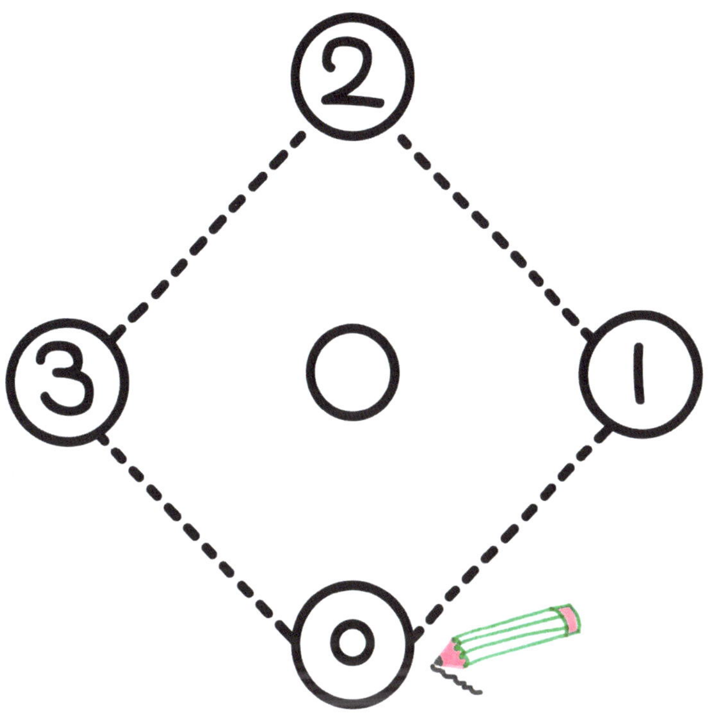

Basketball

Can you **draw along the dotted line** to score a basket?

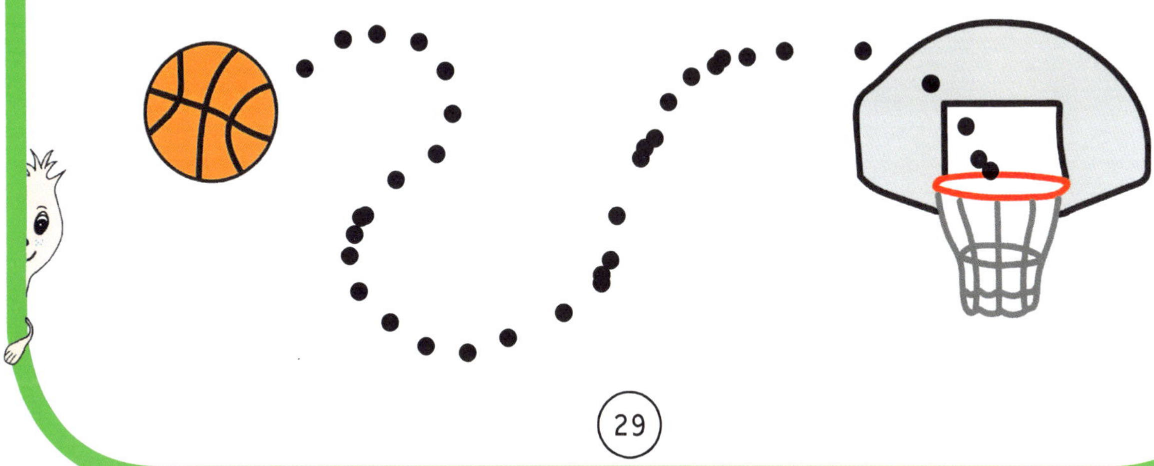

Hollywood

Hollywood is famous for being the home of movie stars and film making. The Oscars Ceremony is held once a year and the best actors and actresses win trophies for their hard work.

Can you **find your way** through the maze from the limousine to the Oscars' trophy?

The Walk of Fame

Along Hollywood Boulevard is the Walk of Fame - where stars appear in the pavement to remember the many famous actors, actresses and singers of the entertainment industry.

Can you **write your name** on this star below? Would you like to be famous one day?

Cowboys

Cowboys have been looking after cattle for centuries and still do today. If you visit the western states you might be able to visit a ranch and see real cowboys at work.

Trace around the lasso to help the cowboy catch the cow.

FACT!
Cowboys wore a bandana to keep the dust out of their noses and mouths

Cowboy Colours

A cowboy has ordered a brand new hat and boots but has forgotten to tell the shop keeper what colour he wants them.

Can you **add some colour** to his hat and boots below?

Shape-search

Find as many of these 3 shapes in the grid as you can:

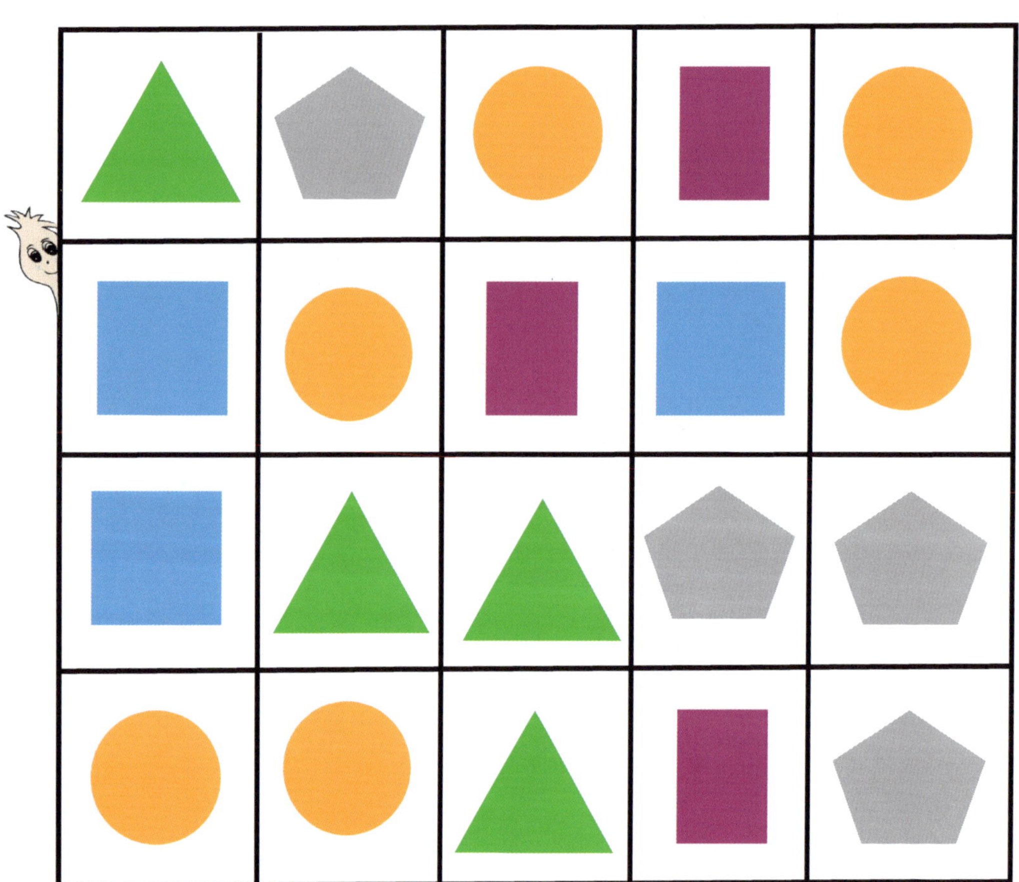

Letter-search USA

Find as many of these 3 letters in the grid as you can:

u__ s__ a__

u	a	a	s	o
s	s	s	c	u
e	o	a	u	s
a	s	u	u	f

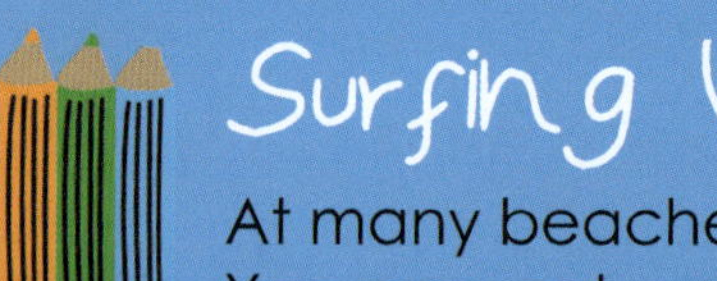

Surfing USA

At many beaches around America's coastline, surfing is a popular sport. You may get a chance to try surfing during your visit.

Design your own surfboard using the template below:

Surfboard Spot the Difference

In each row of surfboards **circle** the one that's different:

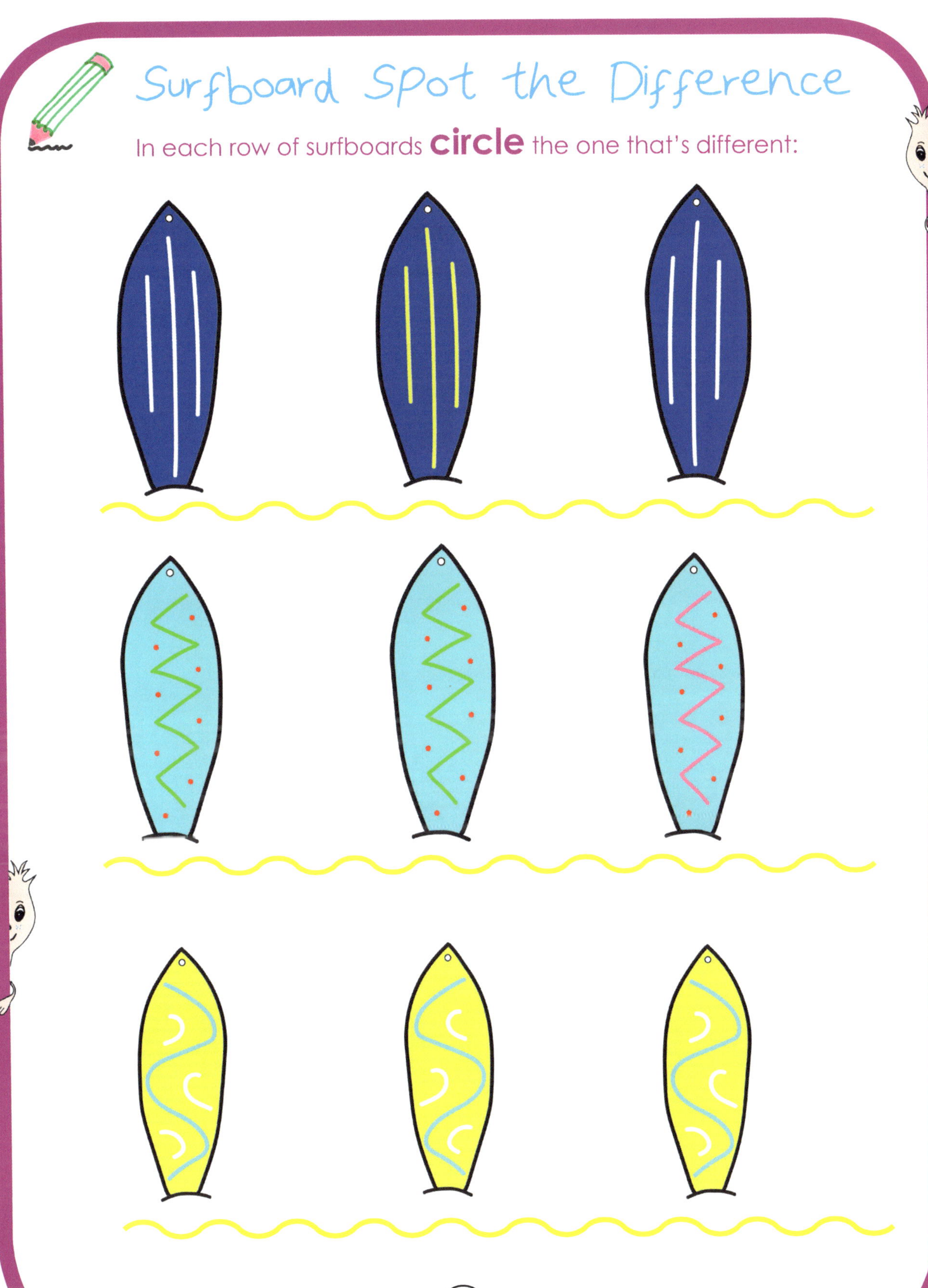

Juke Box Spot The Difference

Rock and Roll music and dancing is very popular in America.

See if you can **spot the 5 differences** between these two juke boxes:

What is your favourite song?

A Place to Stay

Where are you staying on your holiday in the USA? Is it a hotel? A house? A tent? A boat? A campervan? An apartment?

Can you **draw a picture** of it here?

Home Sweet Home

Can you **draw a picture** of where you live back at home?

What is different about this and your holiday home?

What can you remember?

Can you **circle** some of the things you might see in the USA?
Which things do you think you might NOT see?

Memory Bank

Use this section to record and remember all the things you've done, seen and tasted on your trip!

You may need a grown up to help with some of the writing...

What have you eaten?

Draw some food you have eaten on holiday on the plate below. What was your favourite?

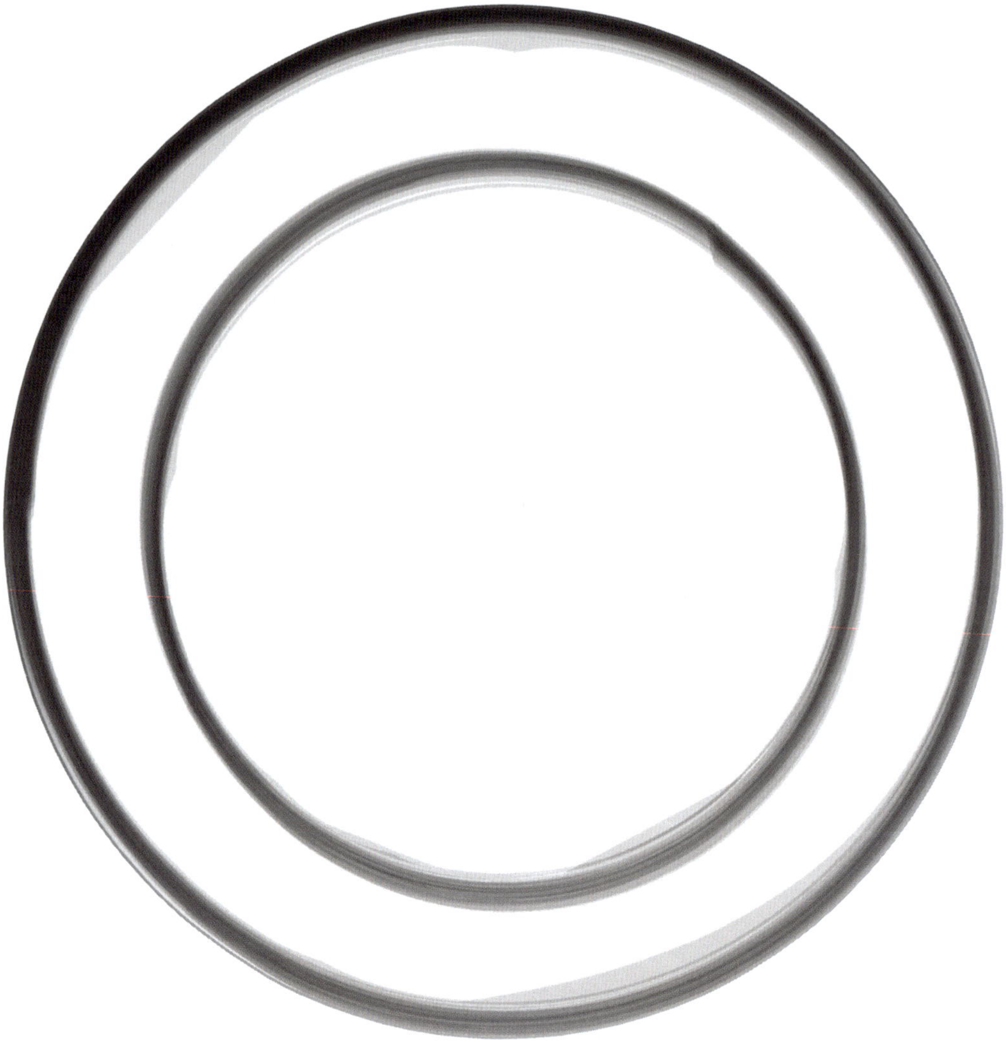

What adventures have you had?

Ask someone to help you **write a postcard** about your adventures, and design a nice stamp:

Carte Postale

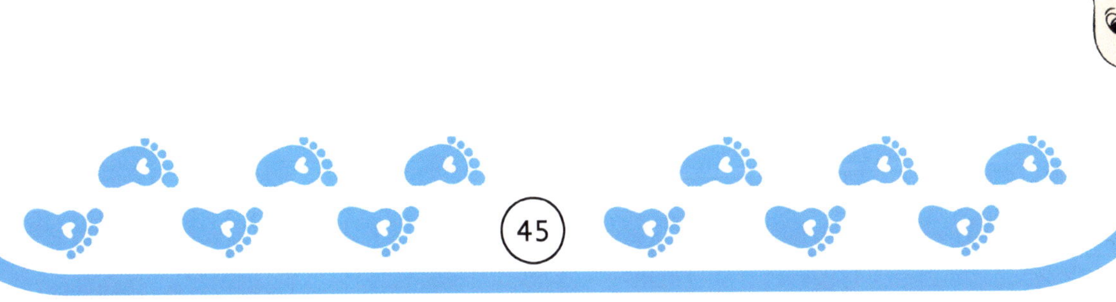

Momento Collage

Stick bits and pieces on these pages that you've collected during your trip; favourite tickets, receipts, leaflets, drawings, flowers...

Daily Diary

Note down some of the different things you have done each day:

Monday

Tuesday

Wednesday

Thursday

Friday

Saturday

Sunday

Memory Gallery

Draw pictures or doodles of any special memories:

Worst 5

What have been the **worst** five things about your trip?

Top 5

What have been the **best** five things about your trip?

Index

(what's in this book and where you can find it)

Goodbye

(until next time)

Keep safe!
Love from
Topher xx

Where would you like to go next?

Spain

Italy

Greece

France

Egypt

China

UK

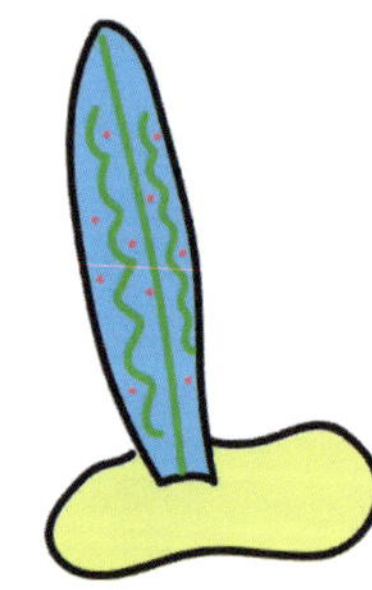

Australia

South Africa

Thailand

Mexico

Finland

Printed in Great Britain
by Amazon